35 Ways to Discover a Major

Kathleen Hartman
Kutztown University

HOUGHTON MIFFLIN COMPANY   BOSTON   NEW YORK

Publisher: Carrie Brandon
Sponsoring Editor: Shani Fisher
Marketing Manager: Edwin Hill
Development Editor: Julia Giannotti
Editorial Assistant: Amanda Nietzel
Marketing Assistant: Bettina Chiu
Editorial Assistant: Jill Clark
New Title Project Manager: Susan Peltier

Printed in the U.S.A.

ISBN 10: 0-547-05230-8
ISBN 13: 978-0-547-05230-4

123456789-CRS-11 10 09 08 07

Table of Contents

Section I
Starting Your Journey toward a Major

Introduction

Welcome to your journey toward deciding what college major is right for you. This book is designed to help you on that journey, which is one of self-discovery, exploration, experiences, and decisions. Being an undecided, undeclared, or exploratory student is not negative; in fact, entering college without a declared major can be one of the smartest decisions you will make in your college career. Deciding that you need more time and information to decide is far better than changing majors too many times or declaring a major that does not suit you. You will be able to research your options through a variety of learning experiences, which will give you the information you need to make the best decision for you. College is a time to discover who you are, what you love, where you want to go, and, ultimately what major is right for you. Deciding on the right major is a journey, but it is one well worth taking.

Activity 1: Why Are You Undeclared?
A "Reality Check" List

A good place to start on your journey to discovering a major may be looking at the reason or reasons why you entered college without a declared major. There is no right or wrong reason for being undecided on a major, and for every college student searching for the right major, there may be just as many reasons. Knowing some of those reasons, however, can tell you more about yourself and help you decide what steps you can take to make a good decision. Read Lynn's story:

Lynn's Story	A Journey to a Major

Lynn came to college undecided for several reasons, none of which made her anxious. In fact, she chose to come to college without a declared major because she felt it was more important to get to know herself better and explore all her options. She always loved school and was really looking forward to taking as many courses in different areas as possible. In high school, she was on the debate team, in the cast of several plays, and on the newspaper staff. She knew she wanted to do something that involved communication. Through a first-year seminar course for undeclared students, she learned about the many possibilities for courses within the communications field. She took an introductory business course, a speech course, and a writing course, all of which helped her explore her options.

During her first year of college, she became a campus tour guide and also spoke to incoming undeclared students about the services available to them. She was a natural in front of groups and really liked to help people. After considering majors in business, speech communication and professional writing, she very happily decided to major in secondary education/communications, which focuses on English, speech, and theater. She is looking forward to teaching, but also knows that her communication skills will open doors in the business world as well.

Step 1: Looking at Your Own Reasons

To get started, complete the "reality check" list below. Check off each reason for being undeclared that applies to you.

_____   I have no idea what I want to do.

_____   I have several ideas, but I need more information about my options before I decide.

_____   I like many things and cannot settle on just one area.

_____   I want to do one thing, but my parents want me to do another.

_____   I think I know what I would like to major in, but I do not know if I have the ability or if I will be happy.

_____   I am not sure that my interests connect to majors that will allow me to get a job or make a good salary.

_____   I did not get into the major of my first choice.

_____   My teachers have always encouraged me to major in a certain area because I am good at it, but I am not sure I agree with them.

_____   I went to college because I thought it is what I should do, but I don't have any idea what to do now.

Step 2

Answer the following questions:

1. Does your reason(s) make you anxious? Why or why not?

_____

_____

_____

_____

_____

2. What do you think you should do now based on your reason(s) for being undeclared?

_____

_____

_____

_____

_____

3. Based on the most significant reason you checked for being undeclared, fill out the diagram below:

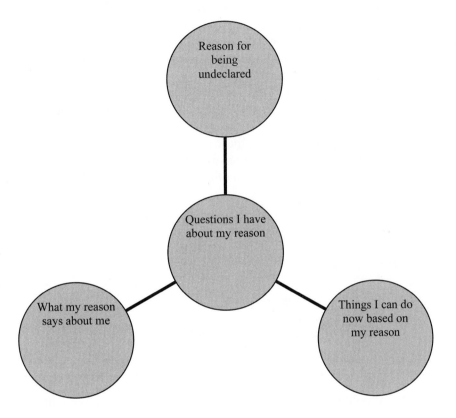

Group Activity:

Share your diagram with at least one other classmate. Share your thoughts and try to help each other with ideas about where to go from here.

Activity 2: Who Are You?

What do you already know about yourself? Taking the time to really answer this question will help you in several ways. First, thinking about this question will allow you to realize that you do have specific likes and dislikes, which can help you make good decisions. Second, just the process of getting down on paper things you know about yourself will help you as you start to answer more questions and complete more activities in this book. Finally, knowing who you are as a person will help you decide what majors seem to "fit" with who you are and those that don't. Also, answering these questions can be very enjoyable. You may also want to share your answers with some of your classmates so that you can get to know each other better and see what you may have in common.

Step 1

"Twenty Questions"

Answer the following questions:

1. What is your favorite food? Why? _____

    _____

2. Would you try a totally strange and new food if you could? If so, what would it be? If not, why not?_____

    _____

3. What types of movies do you like? Why?_____

    _____

4. What type of music do you like to listen to? Why?_____

    _____

5. What do you like to do in your free time?_____

_____

6. What is your favorite place to be? Why?_____

_____

7. What are your friends like?_____

_____

8. What would you read about if you could choose what to read instead
    of being assigned what to read? Why?_____

_____

9. What job have you had that you liked? Why?_____

_____

10. What job would you do if you did not have to worry about money?
    Why?_____

_____

11. Do you like spending time outdoors? If so, why? And what outdoor
    activities do you like? If not, why not?_____

_____

12. Do you like board games, chess, crossword puzzles or other similar
    activities? Why or why not?_____

_____

13. Do you like to work on a task independently or with someone else?
    Why?_____

_____

14. Can you figure out how something works by reading the directions, or do you need someone to explain the directions and show you how to do it? Why?_____

_____

15. Will you plan what you will do on the weekend, or do you enjoy spur-of-the-moment activities? Why?_____

_____

16. What is your favorite season of the year? Why?_____

_____

17. Are you at ease in front of a group of people? If so, why? If not, why not?_____

_____

18. What were your favorite subjects in high school? Why?_____

_____

19. What were your least favorite subjects in high school? Why?_____

_____

20. In what extracurricular activities did you participate while you were in high school? What are you involved in now?_____

_____

Step 2

Students may often think of majors and careers as totally separate from things they like to do for fun or from their likes and dislikes outside of the classroom. In reality, bridging the gap between who you are and what you do will help you find a major and career that best suits you. While every question you answered above will not directly lead you to a decision about a major or career, each question is a start on the journey to learning more about yourself. And the more you know about yourself, the easier it will be to make decisions about a major and possible careers.

Read Bryce's story:

Bryce's Story	**A Realization**

Bryce came to college undeclared and had no idea what he wanted to do with his life. He did not love school as a whole, but he always enjoyed classes in which he could do hands-on activities. He did not know where to start in terms of exploring majors. What he did not realize, however, was that he already knew a lot about himself that could prove useful in helping him start the exploration process. He is a very social person. He likes doing things with friends, from playing in a band to playing volleyball on the weekends. Winter has always been his favorite season of the year, and he has always made the most of winter, from snowboarding and skiing to just enjoying each snowfall. When he has a chance to read anything outside of the reading required for his courses, he reads skiing magazines and keeps up with the latest in computer software and video games. When he plays video games, he likes multiplayer games, especially those that involve racing. Realizing he already had information to start with, he began looking into careers that revolve around skiing. He also looked into majors that are creative and hands-on, like industrial design and product design. Since he likes to be active, he investigated the possibilities of majors related to exercise or sports and leisure studies. He also learned that he could combine several of these interests. Knowing a little about himself was another starting point for Bryce on his journey of exploration toward choosing a major.

Now, it is time to connect what you know about yourself to things you could possibly do in the future. Fill out the chart below by listing some of the things you learned about yourself (from answering the "twenty questions") in the left column. In the right column, without trying to think too hard (just try some free association!), write down possible majors and career paths that come to mind based on each thing you wrote about yourself.

Something about Me	Where It Can Lead

Group Activity:

Share what you wrote in the chart with a small group. Give each other ideas about majors and career paths based on what each person discovered about himself or herself.

Activity 3: When Have You Felt Successful?

Step 1

Look back on things that have happened to you, things you have done, goals you have met, and achievements that have made you proud. When have you felt the most successful? When have you felt confident, knowing that you did a great job? Take some time to think about these questions, and then write your answers below.

_____

_____

_____

_____

_____

_____

_____

_____

_____

Step 2

Now, try to link things that have made you proud to majors and/or careers. Try not to think too hard about this. Use free association, keeping in mind that you have just started the search and you do not know all the majors and careers out there! Just list some majors and careers that come to mind based on what you wrote above.

1. _____

2. _____

3. _____

4. _____

5.   _____

6.   _____

7.   _____

8.   _____

9.   _____

10. _____

Step 3

Why did you write the majors/careers above? How do you think they are related to successes you have had or things you have done that have made you proud? There are no right or wrong answers. Just write your own thoughts.

_____

_____

_____

_____

_____

_____

Group Activity:

Break into small groups to create a "success poster." Have each student share a success story, and then help each other make links to a major and career. Put each person's success and suggested major and career on the poster to share with the rest of the class.

Activity 4: What Do You Fear?

Being afraid is a natural feeling. Everyone is afraid of something to some degree. Very few, if any, people can say they are totally fearless. Take a moment to think of some things that frighten you. Think outside of school and majors at this point. Just think about some things that make you scared or that you would rather avoid. Some people fear flying, while others fear spiders, riding on roller coasters, or speaking in front of a group.

Step 1

Try to think of three things that to some degree make you afraid. Then, think about why. Write your answers in the spaces provided below.

1. I am afraid of:
    _____

    Because:
    _____

    _____

    _____

2. I am afraid of:
    _____

    Because:
    _____

    _____

    _____

3. I am afraid of:

_____

Because:

_____

_____

_____

Step 2

Now, try to think of what you are afraid of in terms of **choosing a major**. Write down your fears in the space below.

_____

_____

_____

_____

_____

_____

_____

_____

_____

Group Activity:

Share your fears with one other person and have him or her offer suggestions for how to ease those fears. Then, switch roles.

Alternative activity:

Write your fears down on a piece of paper and give the paper to your instructor. Ask him or her to offer advice in writing.

Activity 5: What Do You Value?

Values are very personal. They are based on feelings you have, how you have been raised or conditioned, or experiences you have had, both positive and negative. Values relate to everything from making moral decisions to what kind of car you want to drive. Values can shape your life in so many different ways. Some people may value money, while others value time to pursue personal interests. Some people value helping others, while other people may value working alone. Some people value creativity, while others may value order and routine. Almost every aspect of your life is shaped by your values. Values are also very important when making decisions, and they are especially important when making decisions about majors or careers. Sometimes, you may not know everything you value until you are asked to think about it. Take some time now to do just that.

Step 1

What do you value? Write down as many things as you can (from all aspects of your life).

1. _____

2. _____

3. _____

4. _____

5. _____

6. _____

7. _____

8. _____

9. _____

10. _____

Step 2

What does your list say about you?

_____

_____

_____

_____

_____

Step 3

Think about going to work every day when you graduate from college. What do you want in a job? (Think about things such as salary, work hours, work environment, etc.) Be specific when you write your list.

Things that are important to me in a job:

1. _____

2. _____

3. _____

4. _____

5. _____

6. _____

7. _____

8. _____

9. _____

10. _____

Group Activity:

In small groups, share what you wrote above. Ask your classmates in your group for ideas about what types of jobs may meet the criteria you have shared. Each person should have a chance to share and ask for ideas.

Activity 6: Connecting Values to Majors and Careers

Now that you have had time to reflect on what you value, take the time to connect what you value to possible careers that are right for you. If you value time with family and friends, for example, you may be unhappy in a job that requires you to travel the majority of the time. If you value the beauty of nature, you may be unhappy in a career that requires you to live in a major urban center; however, you may be a lot happier in a career that takes you outside or allows you to live in the mountains or near a beach. If you value creativity and personal freedom, you may be much happier working as a freelance writer or photographer than working in a staff position at a newspaper or magazine that would require you to go to work every day in the same place with the same hours. If you value public service, you may be happiest volunteering in college (and there are many opportunities to do so!), majoring in political science or social work (just to name two possibilities), and then perhaps getting into politics or working with troubled youth.

Step 1

In the left column of the table below, write down the values you listed in activity 5. In the right column, try to think of a major and related career you feel can be linked to that value. In other words, what careers would you feel good about pursuing based on your own values? What careers will allow you to do what you value?

Value	Major/Career

Step 2

Do some research on two of the majors/careers you wrote in the previous table. Find out if you are correct in your assumptions that those careers will allow you to pursue what you value and do not conflict with what you value.

Group Activity:

Volunteer to write the careers you researched on the board. Have other people write the careers they researched as well. As a class, discuss the careers in terms of values. Ask yourselves, "What values would a person have who is interested in _____?" See if you agree. This discussion could lead to interesting new insights about careers. You will learn a lot from other students' perspectives.

Activity 7: What Majors Are Out There? And How Important Is a Major Anyway?

As you complete the activities in the following sections of this workbook, you will come to see that choosing a major does not have to be as daunting a task as you think, nor does such a choice determine your career path for the rest of your life. Now is the time to explore options. Now is the time to discover what you love, what you want to learn, who you are. Yes, you will eventually choose a major, but you will hopefully do so with a better sense of what that major really means for you and for your life.

Some of you may be thinking that you don't even know about the possible majors that are out there for you to explore. First, make a list of some of the obvious majors – the ones you do know about.

1. _____

2. _____

3. _____

4. _____

5. _____

6. _____

7. _____

8. _____

9. _____

10. _____

It is also important to learn about majors and career fields you may have never known existed. Do not limit yourself to only the majors that are familiar to you now; be open to all the possibilities by learning how to research majors and determine if you want to find out more about them. These majors may also lead you to related majors or minors that may suit you better. You never know until you begin the search!

Look at the list of majors in the box below. Are you familiar with any of them? What about the ones you are not familiar with?

Some Majors to Explore	What Do You Learn? What Can You Do?
	1. Music Technology 2. Peace Studies 3. Instructional Technology 4. Biostatistics 5. Soil Science 6. Linguistics 7. Industrial Psychology 8. Naval Engineering 9. Gerontology 10. Exercise Science

Asking yourself the questions, "What do you learn?" and "What can you do?" choose two of the above majors you know little or nothing about, but that sound interesting, and research them. What did you discover?

Major 1:

_____

_____

_____

_____

Major 2:

_____

_____

_____

_____

Continue to be open to other possible majors and careers and seek them out as well. (You will learn about more majors and careers as you complete the activities in this book.)

Group Activity:

Share what you learned about these majors in small groups. Discuss additional major and career possibilities so that you can help each other begin the exploration process.

How Important Is a Major Anyway?

Hopefully, after completing the activities in the first section of this workbook, you will see that choosing a major is a journey, one that will lead you to learn more about yourself, about majors, and about the many careers that may be open to you. You may feel overwhelmed by the need to eventually choose a major, but there are a few things to keep in mind. First of all, you need to find out what you really love. You will always do much better in a major that fits who you are. Secondly, you do not have to settle on one major. You can double major, or declare a major and a minor (or more than one minor!), or you may even be able to design your own major. Finally, your college major may lead you to your first job out of college, but it will never determine the rest of your life. Many majors can lead you in different directions, and you can always change career paths as you grow and change as a person. The real-life stories in Section II, Activities 8 and 9, will show you how true this is.

Section II
Breaking Down Preconceived Notions about Majors and Careers

Activity 8: "What's My Major?"

Step 1

After reading the following true-life stories about what people do in their jobs, try to guess each person's undergraduate major. Consult the **"Major Bank"** below to do so. Each person's major is represented there. You may use a major more than once.

Case Study 1: *The Real Estate Appraiser*

My name is Donna, and I am a certified real estate appraiser. My job involves going out to clients' homes or properties, measuring the interior and exterior of the home, taking photographs, determining the age of the property, and completing an interior and exterior inspection. When I am finished at the client's site, I return to the office to write a report. My clients are usually banks, but real estate appraisal is also used in divorce settlements, to find the value of a home someone wishes to place on the market, or in estate sales when a person has passed away. After the report is finished, I am able to give my client the market value of a home or other property. I also appraise small income properties such as two unit and four unit apartment buildings.

What is Donna's undergraduate major?

_____

Case Study 2: *The Software Test Engineer*

My name is Ray, and I am a software test engineer. My job entails testing software before it is released to make sure there are no bugs or problems and that the software works as intended. I have responsibility for setting up the test environment, loading and configuring the software, and setting up the hardware. I am also responsible for documentation under FDA regulations since I work for a company involved in the medical field. This involves working closely with the software developers to ensure that my test plans provide testing coverage of all the specified functional and system requirements. I provide feedback as well as concrete inputs into improved product functionality through my own experiences during the testing process. This makes me an active participant of the development team and often includes direct interactions with our customers. Since the software industry is ever-changing, I must keep abreast of technological changes to ensure I can effectively communicate with other department members as well as prepare thorough testing procedures. I enjoy this aspect of my job, as I am inquisitive by nature. I've found that being a good test engineer involves continually questioning what is already known and maintaining a desire to produce a bug-free product.

What is Ray's undergraduate major?

_____

Case Study 3: *The Oracle Software Consultant*

My name is Ken, and I am an Oracle software consultant. I manage
Oracle Financials implementation and help companies redesign their
accounting systems. Since I am a consultant, I do not work for one
company; rather, I travel around the country, spending time in one
company and then another, as their needs dictate. I enjoy the variety that
my job brings. Even though I manage the same software in each
company, I enjoy doing so at companies that do very different things.
When I first go to work at a company, I document how they are presently
doing business, what they want, and how they want their company to be
run in the future, from financials to accounts payables and receivables.
After this, it is my job to rewrite all of their policies and procedures and
then map them into Oracle. After this, I need to retrain all of their users
and key employees. I will then stay at the company for about another
month, helping them with their day-to-day activities – helping them with
check runs, bringing in and checking invoices, balancing off to the
general ledger, and then closing to the general ledger. I need to be
adaptable to new environments and comfortable meeting new people.

What is Ken's undergraduate major?

_____

Case Study 4: *The Logistics Agent*

My name is Karen, and I am a logistics agent. A logistics agent is
someone who can be seen as a "global coordinator." I work in-house at a
producer of specialty alloys. An alloy is a combination of two or more
elements, one being a metal, with the resulting product having metallic
properties. Some alloys you may be familiar with are steel, brass, and
pewter. These alloys are used in many products made by companies all
over the world. I am responsible for coordinating shipments of our
specialty alloys from domestic distribution centers to customers in other
countries across Europe, in Canada, and in Mexico. Part of my day is
spent looking at emails from the international sales offices and taking
information in order to route shipments properly. I also need to schedule
trucks to pick up and coordinate with personnel in distribution centers to
make sure that the shipments get where they are going. I also must

prepare export documentation for shipments to leave the United States and enter into customs in foreign destinations. My job requires me to be able to coordinate and handle many tasks at once, to keep track of orders, and to deal with external factors influencing the shipments I am coordinating. This can be a challenge, but I love challenges. If I do my job well, the alloys get where they need to be when they need to be there, and my company and our customers are happy.

What is Karen's undergraduate major?

_____

Case Study 5: *The HR Analyst*

My name is Mark, and I am a Human Resources analyst at a state hospital. One of my responsibilities is to administer the Family and Medical Leave Act, making sure that employees can exercise their rights under the act, but also making sure that they do not abuse it. I do labor relations work with supervisors to make sure they are not infringing on the rights of their employees, but I also help them when they need to discipline an employee. Writing skills are an important part of my job, and I find that I write quite often. One of the projects I recently worked on was drafting and sending a letter to all licensed occupational therapists in the county in which our hospital is located. We are having trouble recruiting occupational therapists, so I needed to pitch to my audience the benefits of working at this hospital. In my job as an HR analyst, I interact with people on a daily basis, acting as a source of information, a mediator, a publicist, an organizer, and a report writer, just to name a few of my responsibilities. What I like about my job is that I am able to do many different things, allowing for my creativity and communication skills to be put to good use. I guess this is why I find my job particularly satisfying.

What is Mark's undergraduate major?

_____

The Major Bank	(In Alphabetical Order)
Accounting	Interior Design
Bible	Journalism
Biology	Landscape Architecture
Business Administration	Math
Chemistry	Music
Communication Design	Psychology
Computer Science	Physical Therapy
Elementary Education	Social Work
Engineering	Special Education
English	Theater

Step 2

Now read the same people's stories of how the skills they learned help them in their current careers. Again, using the "**Major Bank**," try to guess what major would best help a person gain the skills described. Then identify which person from the case studies has those skills and is using them on the job.

Skills gained from degree

1. My degree helps me in my job because it gave me the skills needed to deal with people and juggle many tasks at one time. I have learned that it is much easier to get people to do what you want them to do with kindness and respect. I also know how to train people well, so I have had the opportunity to work with new employees, getting them acclimated to the company and to their everyday responsibilities.

Major?

_____

Name?

_____

2. What I studied in college had a great impact on my life. It was what I wanted to do at the time. I was intensely interested in my major then, and I still am. I learned the skills necessary to work with my peers and

customers with whom there may be friction because of disagreements. I am able to help people get along, really listen to what they have to say, and avoid conflicts by being patient and understanding.

Major?

_____

Name?

_____

3. I chose my major in college because it is what I love to do. Because of my major, I have gained valuable problem-solving skills, the ability to think clearly and creatively, and the confidence to interact with people. I use my degree outside of my job as well, working on my own projects. I am good with words, and I have excellent organizational skills.

Major?

_____

Name?

_____

4. My degree helps me in my job because I need to speak the language of my clients, gaining their confidence as I suggest changes in how they do business. Through my degree, I have gained the ability not just to understand what people do in the corporate world, but also to communicate with customers and help them find solutions to problems.

Major?

_____

Name?

_____

5. What I studied in college helps me every day in my job. Because of my degree, I am good with numbers, understand angles and how to measure things, and can apply geometry. I also am able to think quickly,

make accurate calculations, summarize information, and write in a logical and clear manner.

Major?

_____

Name?

_____

Step 3

Finally, complete the table below to the best of your ability.

Name/Career	Skills Needed for Job	Major
Donna Real Estate Appraiser		
Ray Software Test Engineer		
Ken Oracle Software Consultant		
Karen Logistics Agent		
Mark Human Resources Analyst		

Step 4

- Look at your table. Why do you think you completed it the way you did? Do you see any crossover between skills, majors, and careers? In other words, can someone other than the person currently in the job also fit in that career? Why?

_____

_____

_____

_____

- What do your answers tell you about majors and careers?

_____

_____

_____

_____

- What have you learned that you did not know before?

_____

_____

_____

_____

Group Activity:

Before you find out the real answers, get into small groups and compare your own answers with your classmates' answers. How do your answers compare? Why did you get different answers? Listen to what your classmates have to say about how and why they arrived at their answers.

Activity 9: Another Round of "What's My Major?" with a Twist

Here are a few more stories about real people in real jobs. The twist here is that the people represented in this activity have switched careers more than once along the way to their current jobs. Their stories are interesting and provide inspiring proof that your undergraduate major does not determine the one and only path you will follow for the rest of your life. You never know where your undergraduate major will lead you.

Step 1

After reading the following true-life stories about people's journeys through different careers, try to guess each person's undergraduate major. Consult the same **"Major Bank"** on page 26 to do so. Each person's major is represented there. You may use a major more than once.

Case Study 1: *Faculty Advisor for Undeclared Students*

My name is Kelly, and I advise undeclared college students, helping them choose majors and succeed in college. I also teach first-year seminar courses and have written a textbook and workbook for first-year and undeclared students. These books have allowed me to use my writing and artistic skills. In my day-to-day job, I need to have patience and understanding for what students are going through, as well as the knowledge to help them and the ability to communicate with them so that they will be able to work with me to meet their goals. My job has been very rewarding, and certainly never boring! Being a faculty advisor is not what I set out to do after college. I always thought I wanted to work in advertising or for a public relations firm. Right after college, I did work in a corporate, in-house publications office, but I found that my job was lacking the social aspect I needed, and I felt like I wanted to help people in some way. Soon after, I went into high school teaching. While I was teaching in high school, I had the opportunity to teach a college composition course and found that I really enjoyed working with first-year college students. Since then, I have taught writing, reading, and first-year seminar courses at several colleges. All of these experiences have led me to my current position. While I never set out to do what I am doing now, I feel this is where I belong, and my path to this position seems to make sense.

What is Kelly's undergraduate major?

Case Study 2: *Director of a Nonprofit Organization*

My name is Paul, and I am currently the executive director of Communities in Schools in my state. This nationwide, nonprofit organization helps students stay in school and prepare them for life by connecting schools with community resources. Some of my responsibilities include managing and raising funds, hiring and training staff, coordinating initiatives at local affiliates, establishing and maintaining close working relationships with legislators as well as with committees and commissions addressing the issues of young people and their families, and maintaining linkages with media outlets. I became Executive director after working at a local affiliate, handling fundraising and coordinating programs for the schools. Right out of college, I went to work at a small city newspaper, coordinating the "Newspapers in Education Program," an outreach program designed to help high school students produce quality school newspapers and help grade school and middle school students gain reading and critical thinking skills through reading the newspaper. After a few years in this position, I began to write articles for the local section of the paper and soon began to focus exclusively on local politics. In interviewing local politicians and community leaders about local issues, I made some valuable connections. I eventually left the newspaper to become the communications director for the mayor's office. After a few years in this position, which gave me the opportunity to attend many fundraising events for local charities, I became interested in being a part of the solution to some of the problems in our city. I was offered the position at a local affiliate of Communities in Schools. I have been with the organization for five years now and have moved to the state level, where I feel I can contribute on a much larger scale. I love my job and would not change the path that brought me here.

What is Paul's undergraduate major?

_____

Case Study 3: *Small Business Owner*

My name is David, and I am the owner of a landscaping company. We design and create patios, ponds, and gardens for the high-end housing market. We work directly with developers, builders, or homeowners to offer ideas prior to home construction and then landscape the property after the home is built. We also work with clients to replace the existing landscaping at older homes. I supervise a team of landscape designers and subcontract any work that our in-house landscapers cannot complete. My job allows me to be creative, get out of the office to work outside, meet new people, handle employees and budgets, and see projects from start to finish. When I graduated from college, I began working at a small company that created customized computer software for companies to use to train their employees. After I left that company, I went to work for an advertising agency as an account manager. While I enjoyed meeting people and felt comfortable making presentations, I also enjoyed the creative aspect of advertising. One of our clients was a large chain of stores that sold high-end furniture, rugs, drapes, and other home accessories. In working with this client, I was able to visit many of the stores and became very interested in interior and exterior home design. I became a manager of one of these stores and built up a good clientele. After a few years working with homeowners and builders, I decided to try my hand at my own business. While I was in college, I worked summers for a landscaper, so when a well-established landscaping company was for sale, it seemed like a good fit. I love that I am able to combine all of my experiences and abilities in this job. It is also great being my own boss and using my skills to grow the business in new and creative ways.

What is David's undergraduate major?

Step 2

Answer the following questions about the people in the above case studies:

1. How did their *majors* help them in all of their careers and in leading them to their current one?

_____

_____

_____

_____

_____

2. How did their *experiences* help them? (Provide specific examples)

_____

_____

_____

_____

_____

3. Were you surprised by the answers? Why or why not?

_____

_____

_____

_____

_____

4. What did you learn from this activity?

_____

_____

_____

_____

_____

Group Activity:

Before you find out the real answers, get into small groups and compare your own answers with your classmates' answers. How do your answers compare? Why did you get different answers? Listen to what each person has to say about how and why they arrived at their answers.

Activity 10: Doing What You Love: A Myth or a Real Possibility?

Many students believe that what they love to do is not something they can also do to make a living. Where does this belief come from? Many people who love to paint, for example, envision themselves as "starving artists," but may not realize there are many career possibilities with real income potential. Likewise, students who love sports often dismiss the possibility of a career in the field because they "are not good enough to play professionally." But what about the many sports-related jobs out there? Can an interest in the Civil War be translated into a career other than teaching history? The answer is yes, and the answers to many of your other questions about careers related to what you love to do are out there if you do a little research. You will be amazed at the possibilities.

Below you will find a flow chart, which you can complete by following these steps:

1. Begin with identifying three things you really love to do. Do not worry about whether they are "realistic" or not. Do not think about jobs yet – just put down things that you love to do.

2. Now, at the next level of the flow chart, after completing some research on you own, identify careers that are related to what you love to do (and that you consider realistic in terms of your own skills, abilities, interests, and goals).

3. At the third level, think about majors that might lead you to those careers. (Remember what you learned from Activity 8, "What's My Major?")

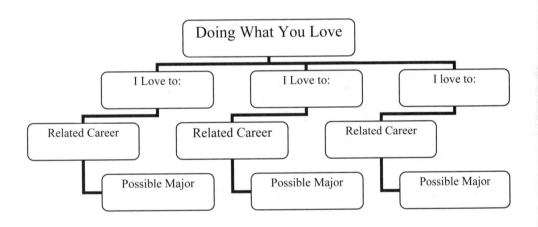

Questions

1. What did you learn from completing this activity?

   _____

   _____

   _____

2. What else can you do now to find out more about career
   opportunities linked to what you love to do?

   _____

   _____

   _____

3. What majors are you interested in after completing this activity?
   Why?

   _____

   _____

   _____

Group Activity:

Find a partner. Take turns being a "career counselor" and a "client."
To do this, the career counselor should ask his or her client the following
questions:

- Which of the three things you love to do would be first on your
  list? Why?

- What career did you find the most interesting? Why?

- Do you believe you identified majors that could lead to such a
  career? What are they?

- What else can you do now to reach this goal, if you decide it is what you might want to do?

Then, the career counselor should offer his or her own ideas of other careers he or she can think of that would relate to the client's interests and make suggestions for reaching goals.

Reverse roles and repeat the process. You may want to share your ideas with a larger group or the whole class. More people means more ideas you may not come up with yourself!

Activity 11: Linking Skills (Not Majors) to Careers

You probably know that many students change majors more than one time. Similarly, many people change jobs and careers several times. Do you think that each time a person changes a career that he or she goes back to school to earn a new degree? Of course we know that this does not always happen; in reality, many people are able to change jobs because of the skills they have (through training and experience). Many people with different college majors end up in the same career because they have similar skills. If you think about skills first, you may be able to expand your thinking about majors and realize that more than one major can help you gain many of the same skills, and that skills, more often than specific majors, are what open the doors to new careers. Thinking this way may help you to worry less about picking the "perfect" major (which can prevent you from picking any major) because there may be more than one major that will lead you where you want to go.

Look at the diagram below. It represents the skills of Krista, a marketing manager for a lacrosse equipment company. The skills identified in the circles surrounding the center circle are ones Krista gained throughout high school, college, and early job experiences. These skills led her to her current job. Notice that her college major is not identified on the diagram. What do you think it was?

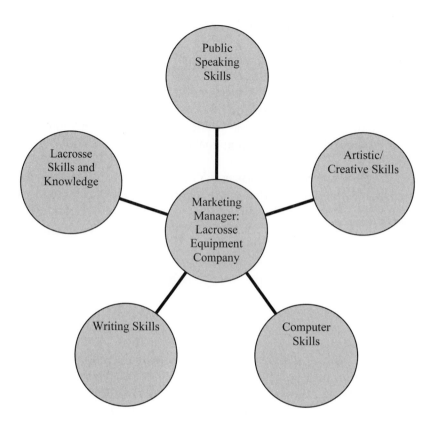

Krista's college major was journalism. She chose this major because she liked to write, and she thoroughly enjoyed her college courses. Yet, she was not specifically set on being a journalist. After graduation, she did not write for a newspaper, television news station, or magazine; rather, she began working at the lacrosse equipment company in an entry-level position before she became their marketing manager. She did not major in marketing, design, public relations, or computer graphics. Having a degree in journalism certainly helped Krista become an excellent writer and communicator. She did, however, learn other important skills that helped her land this job. First, she knows and loves the sport of lacrosse. (Who says you can't get a job in "sports"?) She used the company's equipment throughout her high school and college playing days and really believes in what the company has to offer. She has always had excellent artistic skills. She took a few art courses in college, but she gained more experience with design and computer-based applications through her work on the college's literary magazine. She has always been a social person, and she loves to travel and meet new people. Her experiences and her skills (not specifically her major) led her to what she does now: designing logos and packaging for company merchandising, designing the company catalog, creating trade show visual displays, and working with the advertising agency in creating print and television ad campaigns. She could have landed this job with a degree in marketing or design, just to name a few. It was important that she has a college degree, but her major alone did not get her in the door; her skills did.

There are many majors that can help you gain similar skills, just as there are many experiences that can do so as well. Think about what skills you have and what skills you want to gain *first*. Then go back and think about majors.

Now, think about the skills you currently have (and would like to use!) and those you would like to gain. Write them below:

_____

_____

What jobs/careers can these skills lead you to? (You may need to do a little research.)

_____

_____

Below you will find a blank diagram identical to the one identifying Krista's skills. Write those skills you identified above in the outer circles. When you complete this step, think about the careers you identified above that require these skills or for which these skills would be an asset. Write one or two of these careers in the center circle. Keep majors out of the picture for now. You can put them back in later.

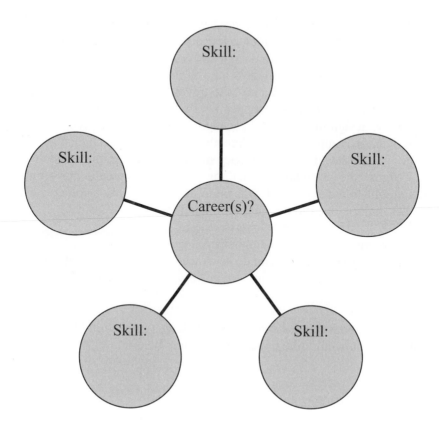

If you think about skills first, you may come to realize that you can, in fact, choose from many majors that will enhance skills you already have or help you gain new ones. Choose a major you will love, not one that will land you a specific job. As you have already learned, there are many majors that lead to the same job, and you do not have to stay in the same career your entire life.

Group Activity:

Interview an administrator, professor, or staff member (such as the registrar, financial aid officer, or student activities director) on your campus. Ask him or her the following questions:

- How did you come to be in your current position? (Can you share your career path, including college and former positions?)

- How does your college major help you in your current position?

- What skills have you gained from your education and your former positions that helped lead you to your current position?

Activity 12: Starting Small, Thinking Big (Linking College Courses to Skills)

In your first year of college, you take many general education courses, especially if you have not yet decided on a major. You may already have decided that you dislike math or that you are not good in science, but this is college, a fresh start, and a time to shake off any old views of courses and look at them anew. You can gain skills from each course you take, even if the course is in an area you never plan on making your major. Also, taking a look at the skills you can gain from courses may help you to see that a major related to one of those courses may be of interest to you. The key is to really think about what you can gain from each course and how you think those skills can be applied not just to other courses, but also to possible careers. Give your first year courses a chance. They may just lead you to a major!

You may be taking a *history* course this semester. Have you thought about how such a course improves your research skills? Research skills are necessary in many career fields. For example, did you know there is such a thing as a *corporate historian?* Corporate historians look at important aspects of companies, such as past products and policies, competitors, and past decisions as they impact future business decisions. Courses in *psychology and sociology* give you a better understanding of human behavior. Careers in fields such as *human resources* and *sales* require just such an understanding. *Math* skills can take you into the *retail sector*, for instance, in areas such as inventory management, analysis of sales data, and future sales forecasting. You have many interesting options.

To begin your own process of looking at your courses in terms of the skills you will gain, complete the table below. Start with writing each of your courses in the rows under the first column labeled "Courses." Then, for each course, write a few skills you have gained or think you will gain from the course. After that, spend some time thinking about how you might apply those skills in the "real world." Write a few of these ideas in the third column. Finally, rate your interest in each course on a scale of 1-5, with 1 being "not at all interested" and 5 being "very interested."

Courses	Skills Gained	How Skills Can Be Applied	Interest in Course

What does your table say about you?

_____

_____

_____

What course(s) interest you the most? Why?

_____

_____

_____

What majors are related to the courses that most interest you? Find out as much as you can about those majors. Talk to your professors and students in those majors.

_____

_____

_____

Group Activity:

Form small groups based on course interest. Each group should represent one course or content area (for example, history, English, biology, etc.) You should join the group based on which course interests you the most. When the groups are formed, the group members should create a visual aid (such as a poster) showing how that course or major relates to skills, majors, and careers. Groups should share their visuals with the class.

Activity 13: Skills and Majors: Many Intersections

Another Look:

Take the skills you identified in the second column in the table you completed in Activity 12. Write them again below. Next to each skill, write the first major that comes to mind when you think about that particular skill.

Skills   Majors

1. _____   _____

2. _____   _____

3. _____   _____

4. _____   _____

5. _____   _____

Now, go back and look at your list of skills again. For each skill, draw a line to any other major on your list that you believe would also help a student develop that skill.

How many majors and skills intersect? Understanding that many majors and skills do intersect may help you realize that choosing a major is not a be all and end all decision. Choose what you love. Choose what you want to learn. The rest will follow.

Group Activity:

Write as many courses (that all your classmates are enrolled in) as possible on the board. Share ideas about what skills students will gain from those courses, then write down the majors associated with those skills. Try to learn as much as you can from each other.

Activity 14: One Product, Many Majors (Taking a Closer Look to See the Broader Picture)

Think about things you own, things you eat, things you do. Most of you probably own a cell phone. Many of you eat cereal for breakfast. Many of you like to play video games. When you use, eat, or experience a product, you may not give a lot of thought to how it came to be or the people who made it possible. Just who is involved in the products you encounter every day? The answers may surprise you. Thinking about things you have or use every day in this context keeps you from having a limited view about where majors can lead you. You will find that you can do a lot more with particular majors than you may have thought possible.

Did you have cereal for breakfast this morning? Say you really like cereal and even have ideas for new types of cereal. The first person you may think of when you think of cereal is someone with a food background, perhaps a culinary arts degree. Maybe you don't see yourself majoring in anything food related, so you give up on some day working for a cereal company. But there are many other people involved in getting a new cereal from an idea to a box on your kitchen table: product tasters, researchers, nutritionists, food scientists, marketing staff, advertising directors, package designers, and many more.

The same is true for cell phones. Say you really love your cell phone and all of the high-tech things it can do. Perhaps you have thought about ways your cell phone could be even better but don't see yourself as a technical person. While it would be easy to think about the people behind cell phones being technically inclined, perhaps having majored in engineering or computer science, such a limited view would leave out the many people with other backgrounds and jobs who also made such a product possible. But what other people were responsible for getting your cell phone to you? If you stop and think about this, you will see that many different people with different college majors may have played a role in making your cell phone a reality. To take a close look at who may be associated with your cell phone, try to think about the many steps it may have taken to produce the final product. Try to list all the people (jobs) that come to mind. Do so by completing the following table. Really think about this. Think about concepts, designs, screen layout, functionality, ease of use, technology, colors, marketing ideas, sales, networks, and technical support.

Below you will find the first person (job title) on the list to get you started. The job title is "ergonomist," and an ergonomist is involved in the design and evaluation of products in order for the product to meet the needs, abilities, and limitations that people have. As cell phones get smaller but more complex, ergonomists play a role in making sure that phones remain "user-friendly." But there are many more people involved in the world of cell phones. As you complete the table, after you come up with each possible job (career) write a possible major in the appropriate space in the second column, as seen in the example below. (You will have to do some research.)

"Cell Phone Careers"

Job Title	Possible Major(s)
Ergonomist	psychology, mechanical engineering, health science, occupational therapy

Now, complete a table for a product of your choice:

Product: _____

Job Title	Possible Major(s)

Group Activity:

After you are done completing your table, compare your answers with your classmates in a small group. See what they thought of that you did not.

Follow-up Activity:

Complete some in-depth research on at least one job related to cell phones that might interest you. If you are thinking, "I'm not interested in cell phones," choose to research a job related to cell phones that is also related to another product.

Activity 15: One Experience, Many Majors (Taking a Closer Look to See the Broader Picture)

Just as you identified a product and the many careers related to it, think now about things you like to do for fun. Do you enjoy going to concerts? Are you a sports fan who likes to go to major league games? Do you try to see new exhibits at art or science museums? Have you always liked the outdoors, taking hiking or camping trips? Do you find watching a Broadway show or local theater production exciting? Whatever it is you enjoy doing, people are involved at many different levels to make your experiences possible. The next time you go to a show or a game, for example, look around you and try to think of the many people working behind the scenes or of the many people who worked before the show or game even got started. To get you thinking, read the following story.

Many Roads Can Lead to Broadway	**One Show, but a Cast of Thousands**

I was seven when I saw my first Broadway show in New York City. After that, I was hooked. I try to see at least one show a year, and I am involved in as many shows on my campus as possible. I am a theater major, although I came to college undecided because I didn't think I could make a living as an actor. At my university, there are many theater-related majors: acting; costume, scenic or lighting design; and production. I now know that the people on stage are only a part of the "cast of thousands" that it takes to put on a Broadway show. Backstage, there are costume designers, interior decorators, and broadcast technicians. On the production end, there are casting directors, company managers, marketing directors, and theatrical press agents, to name a few. I am majoring in acting but with a minor in marketing and set design. I will have a lot of options when I graduate, having had the experiences on stage, but also because of an internship designing and creating sets for a summer theater in my hometown. When you think about it, there are so many opportunities for people who love the theater. Breaking into the field is not as impossible as you may think.

Just as you identified a product and the many careers related to products, now try to identify the many careers (and possible college majors) associated with something you like to do. You may need to do some research.

Event/Activity: _____

Job Title	Possible Majors

Group Activity:

After you are done completing your table, compare your answers with your classmates in a small group. Then, volunteers can report to the entire class about careers they may have never thought of before!

Activity 16: Identifying and Eliminating Stereotypes about Careers

Have you ever thought about stereotypes that exist in terms of careers? Maybe you have been harboring some stereotypes of your own about careers that may be limiting your major exploration. Some stereotypes are mistakenly negative, such as "accountants are conservative and boring," and some may be mistakenly positive, such as "a career in sales will allow me to travel all over the country, which will be very exciting." You will find out, of course, that many accountants are anything but conservative and some don't just crunch numbers at a desk without talking to anyone all day. Likewise, you will find that many people outgrow the charm of travel, when living out of a suitcase and enduring long waits at the airport become a drag. We also may stereotype careers in terms of salaries. Do you think certain jobs pay well while others do not? Do you know the real starting salaries of certain careers, and do you know how long it may take in a given career to reach the salary you may think you get right out of college? Do you think people in careers with lower salaries have less job satisfaction? You need to know the truth. This knowledge can open your mind to careers that you are currently ignoring because of stereotypes. Below is a story of how one person identified and overcame a stereotype about his chosen career.

Hitting the Books	An Unexpected but Happy Ending

When I was in high school, I enjoyed reading novels, and I always did well on research papers. I liked my science courses also, but I never connected all these things to a specific career. Because of this, I entered college undeclared, unsure of what I wanted to major in or what career path to take, although I always thought I would enter the business world. During my freshman year, I was going through the required general electives, not giving much thought to why I was taking them. That was, until I signed up for a course called "Libraries in the Information Age." I had dropped another course at the last minute, and that was the only course available at a time that would fit my schedule. Before it even started, I bought into the stereotype of librarians as geeky old maids with glasses and their hair in buns, telling everyone to be quiet. When the class started, however, my stereotype was shattered. With the wealth of information now available, librarians need to be technologically savvy. I was surprised at how much technology was available in my college library. Through this course, I learned that there was such a thing as a corporate librarian. Sometimes known as information specialists or knowledge managers, corporate librarians work for pharmaceutical, legal, and medical companies, locating and organizing competitive information and even researching potential clients and candidates for executive positions. I declared library science as a major and chemistry as a minor, and, after also receiving a master's in library science, I was offered a position as an information scientist doing research in a major pharmaceutical firm. I never would have known about careers in library science had it not been for that first course. I love my job, am paid well, and am always challenged with new projects.

Below you will find a list of careers. Write your own stereotypes about each of those careers, being as honest as possible.

1. Dermatologist_____

   _____

2. Reporter_____

   _____

3. Physical Education Teacher_____

   _____

4. Social Worker_____

   _____

5. Accountant_____

   _____

6. Engineer_____

   _____

Now, interview at least one person in one of the above careers and find out the "real story."

You can also research the typical job duties, job environment, and salary of a person in one of the above careers (or another career for which you may have a stereotype) by searching the Internet or visiting your campus career services office.

Group Activity:

1. Get into small groups and write all the stereotypes the members had for each career on a piece of poster board. When your group is done, hang the poster somewhere in the room. Assign a group spokesperson. Each group will take turns reporting the groups' stereotypes. This will give the whole class an opportunity to see what others think and to discuss these stereotypes as a way to begin breaking them down to get to the real truth.

2. Work with a partner or small group to research one career from the list, profiling at least one real person working in that field and providing information about job duties, working environment, salaries, and employment outlook. Share your findings with the class.

3. Another Quick Guessing Game: For another look at the many places a major can take you, try to guess the majors of the famous people below:

    1. Jon Stewart
    2. Oprah Winfrey
    3. Sandra Day O'Connor
    4. Robin Williams
    5. Brooke Shields
    6. Yo-Yo Ma
    7. Sally Ride
    8. Paul Newman

Conclusion

Now that you have completed the activities in this section of the workbook, reflect on whether or not you have been able to break down your own preconceived notions about majors and careers. If you have been able to break down even one of your own preconceived ideas, you are now more open to looking at majors differently and perhaps taking a new look at majors you may not have thought about before. Remember that it is not your major that defines you. Decide what you want to know, what you want to learn, what you love to do. Then look at what majors will get you there. Careers will come later...and who knows what those careers might be.

Section III
Finding the Real Answers to "What Do/Will I Love to Do?"

Activity 17: Your Own Interest/Course/Major Matrix: A Look at Many Intersections on the Road to a Major

Sometimes you need to take a closer look at what is important to you in order to find answers to questions about what paths may be right for you. Often, your interests, the courses you enjoy, and possible majors intersect, helping you see possibilities you may not have seen before. This activity will help you see those intersections and connections by using matrices and Venn diagrams. A matrix is a useful tool for categorizing data, and when it comes to interests and courses, categorizing them helps you understand how you feel about them and how they can help you make decisions about majors. A matrix utilizes four quadrants for categorizing information; you will learn the significance of each quadrant in these matrices after you complete this exercise. This activity involves filling in two different 2 x 2 matrices.

Here is an example of how one student completed the first matrix:

As an undecided student, Hannah is taking five general education courses during her first semester in college. She completed the matrix below according to the information requested for each numbered quadrant:

1. Course she likes and finds applicable to her own life and interests

2. Course she likes but does not find applicable to her own life and interests

3. Course she does not like but finds applicable to her own life and interests

4. Course she does not like and does not find applicable to her own life and interests

1 Psychology	2 Geometry
3 Introduction to Forensic Science	4 History of Civilization

Hannah is not yet sure of her major, but she has always had an interest in psychology. She also loves her geometry class but does not see herself in a field requiring math. While she does not like her forensic science course very much, she knows that it relates to her interest in psychology in terms of developing problem-solving skills. Also, if she decides on psychology as a major, she is not sure if she will end up as a psychologist, a psychiatrist, or a school counselor, among other possibilities. This course helps expose her to other areas that may be connected to psychology. Finally, she has never had much interest in ancient history and does not see how this course will help her in the future. She is more interested in people and in the present.

Hannah then completed the second matrix below according to the information requested for each numbered quadrant:

1. Activity she likes and thinks will help her in the future

2. Activity she likes but does not think will help her in the future

3. Activity she doesn't like but thinks will help her in the future

4. Activity she does not like and does not think will help her in the future

1 Tutoring elementary school students in an after-school program	2 Singing in the chorus
3 Swimming laps in the pool every afternoon	4 Working at the coffee shop on campus

Hannah loves working with children. She also loves to sing but does not see how that will help her find a job. She doesn't really like exercising, but she knows that being disciplined and staying healthy will help her in the long run. She is not sure how working in a coffee shop will help her, but her friend told her that any experience working with people, especially difficult customers, will help her, especially if she majors in psychology.

When she took her course in quadrant 1 from the first matrix and her activity from quadrant 1 in the second matrix, she realized she had just learned a few things about herself. Her favorite course and one she thinks will help her in the future is psychology, while her chosen activity is tutoring children in an after-school program. If she combines both of these interests, she can see a connection to careers as a teacher, guidance counselor, school psychologist, and child psychologist, to name a few. This is a good place for Hannah to get started.

Now, complete the first matrix just as Hannah did. The first matrix is designed to help you categorize some of the courses you are currently taking. Write the information requested below in the corresponding quadrant.

1	2
3	4

1. Course you like and find applicable to your own life and interests

2. Course you like but do not find applicable to your own life and interests

3. Course you do not like but find applicable to your own life and interests

4. Course you do not like and do not find applicable to your own life and interests

The second matrix is designed to help you categorize activities you are involved in on or off campus (clubs, sports, volunteer work, personal pursuits such as hobbies, etc.). Just as Hannah did, write the information requested below this matrix to complete it.

1	2
3	4

1. Activity you like and think will help you in the future

2. Activity you like but do not think will help you in the future

3. Activity you don't like but think will help you in the future

4. Activity you do not like and do not think will help you in the future

As you learned at the beginning of the exercise, a matrix allows for rapid separation of information into four categories.

What is placed in the upper left quadrant has the most desirable characteristics, while what is placed in the lower right quadrant has the least desirable characteristics. Think about your own matrices. What can you learn from what you placed in each quadrant? Now, notice the Venn diagram that follows. Venn diagrams are useful in understanding what seemingly different things have in common. To complete the Venn diagram below, follow the directions beneath it.

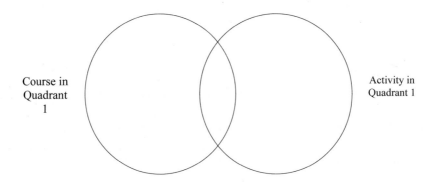

Course in
Quadrant
1

Activity in
Quadrant 1

Fill in the two circles in the Venn diagram above using what you wrote
in each matrix. Then look at where the two circles intersect. What do
your course from quadrant 1 and your activity from quadrant 1 have in
common?

_____

_____

_____

_____

_____

Look at your list of commonalities above. What majors come to mind? Why?

_____

_____

_____

_____

_____

What careers now come to mind? Why?

_____

_____

_____

_____

What can you learn from what you wrote in the other quadrants? Refer back to Hannah's examples for help answering this question.

_____

_____

_____

Group Activity:

Form small groups and share your results. Then, look at what everyone put in quadrant 3. Box three translates into low interest but high applicability. How can you still benefit from the courses and activities you wrote down in quadrant 3? Think about it! Your answers will help you see how everything you do in college can help you get closer to your goals.

Activity 18: Choosing a Reading: What Does It Say about You?

Step 1

Read only the first sentence (in bold) of each of the following paragraphs. (Don't cheat!) Then, go back and finish reading the paragraph that interests you the most. Make a check next to the first sentences that peak your interest as you go, so it will be easier for you to find the paragraph you decide to finish reading.

1. **Mary's mother held her daughter's hand, trying to stop her from crying, hoping she would soon be excited about all the toys, books, and other children in the room.**
It was Mary's first day of kindergarten, a day Mary had been talking about for weeks. She left the house that morning ready to take on the new world of kindergarten. Yet, here she was now, crying nonstop. It was only when her teacher, Mrs. Walker, came over that Mary stopped crying. Mrs. Walker took her by the hand and gave her a tour of the room. She gave her a sticker to put on her shirt and introduced her to another student, Lydia, who was busy completing a puzzle. Lydia was outgoing, pulling Mary down to the floor with her, and soon both girls were busy working on the puzzle together. When she started college, Mrs. Walker was not sure what she wanted to major in, but after taking a job at the campus day care center, she realized she wanted to work with children. The start of every school year has been as exciting for her as for her students, and today was no different. When all the students settled in, Mrs. Walker began to gather the students in a circle, getting ready to play some games that would help the children get to know each other and have fun at the same time. Her students sat down, ready to begin their first day of school, one that they would remember for a long time.

2. **The company management was meeting to select the final design for its new office building.**
Several architectural firms had bid on the project, and they would be speaking with the final two firms still in the running. The first firm

created a building designed around the natural landscape on which it was to be built, utilizing the slope of the land, the native trees, and the lake and small stream running into it. The building was to be largely a glass structure, blurring the lines between the outdoors and the indoors. Each office would be flooded with natural light, with open courtyards in the center of the building that would be small-scale arboretums, where employees could take a brief stroll or eat lunch on tables lining the paths. Mary worked for this firm, and she was one of the principal architects on the project. She loved the building design; it fit the sensibilities of the small, employee-centered medical equipment company. The company encouraged employee health and fitness and also knew the value of an environment in which stress could be reduced. After meeting with both firms over the course of several days, Mary's company won the bid. She felt an overwhelming sense of pride, for she felt a large part of her went into the design of the building.

3. **Carl was trying to convince a roomful of people that his ad campaign was the one they wanted, but his pitch was going poorly.**

He could see from his potential clients' faces that they were tuning him out, looking at their watches, wondering what they were going to have for lunch. Carl felt a more conservative ad campaign would appeal to this insurance company, but, apparently, he was wrong. Luckily, he had an alternate ad campaign idea with him, one he didn't think his potential clients would like, but he realized now that he misread the company's original intentions. They wanted to appeal to younger customers. Within minutes, he had put up a new set of storyboards, showed a very short video, discussed possible slogans, and showed them designs for print ads. The insurance company executives were soon throwing out other ideas, making suggestions for tweaking the slogan, and suggesting possible songs for the television ads. The energy is what Carl loved most about working at an advertising agency. He had felt this way since his first graphic design class. He was a visual person, a creative thinker, but he also wanted the challenge of the business world, so he combined his art degree with a minor in marketing. It was the right decision. His presentation to the insurance company turned around that day, and his potential clients soon became his actual clients. Carl left the meeting ready to begin the process of bringing his ideas to life.

4. **After several hours of surgery, Dr. Williams was tired, but she still had to talk to the patient's family.**

Sometimes talking to a patient's family is the toughest part of her job, but today she could tell the family that the surgery went well. Her patient, Mike, is a retired teacher who has been enjoying his free time with his wife, children and grandchildren. For several months Mike had a cough that would not go away. When Mike visited his primary physician, he was told to go for a chest x-ray, which revealed a suspected tumor on his lung. He then had a CT scan to assess his lungs and entire upper abdomen, which was followed by a fine needle aspiration test to gather cells for a biopsy. The diagnosis of lung cancer was confirmed. Mike had smoked for most of his life, but he had quit about five years before, after becoming a grandfather. He had been eating well and exercising and had been feeling better than he had in a while. This made his diagnosis all the more unsettling. Mike was lucky, however. He had a non-small cell lung cancer that had not spread to his lymph nodes or other parts of his body. Because he had no heart problems and was otherwise healthy, he was a good candidate for surgery. Dr. Williams performed the surgery through a cut around the side of Mike's chest to reach the lung. She then removed the part of the lung containing the tumor. Mike did very well in the surgery, and Dr. Williams was able to tell Mike's wife and children that she believed she got all of Mike's cancer, which is not something she can say to every patient. Mike's recovery from the surgery would be long, but Mike was going to leave the hospital with some hope for the future.

5. **Tim and Valerie had only the decomposing body to work with in this puzzling case.**

The 911 call came in from a group of friends on a hiking and camping trip in New England. They were just a few miles into their hike on the second day when they came upon the body, partially hidden by the overgrown bushes just off the hiking path. Shaken, they called the police and silently waited with their gruesome discovery. That is where Tim and Valerie came in. As investigators, they considered this a crime scene until facts might prove otherwise. First, the area around the body was sealed, then the team began to slowly collect evidence. The first thing Tim and Valerie had to determine was the postmortem interval, the amount of time that has elapsed since the person died. They had to assess the state of decomposition, as well as the state of rigor mortis and algor mortis (or body cooling). They were also able to assess the insect activity on the corpse, which could help them determine the time and location of

the death. The rest of their team was sifting through trace evidence:
fibers, hairs and other materials found on and around the body. Every
piece of evidence was carefully lifted and placed in a sterile, sealed
container to be analyzed in the crime lab. Trying to identify the body
would be next. Meanwhile, the hikers were interviewed, and the police
began investigating any leads that might fill in the blanks in this case.
Tim and Valerie were a long way from solving the mystery, but
mysteries are part of their job.

6. **After another day of copyediting another author's work, Rachel
realized she had enough.**
It was not that she wasn't good at copyediting. She has always loved
English, and she is very good at correcting errors in grammar, spelling,
usage, and style. Yet, because of these skills, she knew that she was also
a good writer. She wanted to be published. She had been working at
Sophisticated Style, a fashion magazine, for more than three years, right
after graduating with a degree in English with a minor in creative
writing. She has always been a "clothes horse," so landing a job at this
particular magazine was a dream come true for her. When she took the
job, she knew she had to pay her dues; copyediting was her way into the
business. She has done well at this job, impressing he supervisors with
her dedication and enthusiasm. Since she had established a good
reputation at the magazine, she knew the time was right to give the editor
a few of the articles she had been working on. Soon after, the editor
called Rachel into her office. While the editor did not feel any of the
articles were publication ready, she did see potential in Rachel's writing
and enabled her to work closely with one of the writers. After several
rejections, she finally had an article published – about the role of purses
in women's lives. She was very proud of her accomplishment; she was
realistic about her goals right out of college, and she gained the skills and
experience on the job to finally become a staff writer.

7. **It was opening night, and the restaurant was full, making Rob
both happy and nervous on a day he had waited for as long as he
could remember.**
After earning a business management degree, and after working several
years managing restaurants in Orlando and Atlanta, he was finally able to
open his own restaurant in Philadelphia. It was called River, after his
love of rowing. He was on the rowing team all four years of college and
spent many a day practicing on the Schuylkill River. Of all the
restaurants he had managed, he loved the ones specializing in fresh

seafood, flown in every day from various locations across the globe. He became an expert, learning all about the different types of seafood and how best to prepare them. Salmon was one of his favorites, and it was the star of his new menu. He also loved pairing wines with food and hired an excellent sommelier to help his customers have the best dining experience possible. He designed River himself, hiring architects and designers to bring his vision to life. The décor turned out to be sleek and sophisticated, with blue walls shimmering with silver wall hangings that mimic the flow of a river. As he stood in the doorway leading to the kitchen, listening to the bustling of the chefs and looking out at the wait staff navigating the tables, he knew this is where he belonged.

8.   **After listening to the latest recording of the song, Ian realized they needed to get back to the studio.**
For the last two weeks, his band had been working on their newest CD, and they were happy with the results, except for the last song, which was currently bare and unembellished. Feeling unsatisfied with how the final track had turned out, they sought help from their producer, who suggested adding some vocal harmonies, overdubbing guitars, and adding effects such as reverb to the keyboard part. The band also wanted to take more time to think about the message of the song, the emotional pull. When they went back to the studio, they spliced different tracks together, moved things around, recorded some additional vocals, and changed some of the lyrics. This is what recording a CD was all about. They worked well into the night in the studio, but they became energized by the way the song was turning out. They left that night feeling good about the entire CD. It was a departure from their last CD, but still true to their roots.

9.   **The plane landed at 10 A.M. local time in Sidney, Australia, and Brett was tired as he reached for his laptop, but he had never been to Sidney before, and another adventure awaited him.**
Ever since he graduated with a degree in business, Brett has loved to travel. In his junior year of college he had the opportunity to study abroad in Spain, and his love of travel was born. Brett has never been bothered by the small inconveniences of travel: long lines at the airport, lost luggage, living out of a suitcase. He landed a job in international sales soon after graduation, and his study abroad and language courses helped give him an edge. He loves to meet new people and is a skilled public speaker. He cannot imagine going to work every day in the same office. After traveling to many different countries, Brett was now in

Australia, and he was excited about taking in the sights after his business meetings were over. He had already read many travel books about Sidney and was ready to make the most of his trip as soon as he got off the plane. He would be sure to check out Darling Harbour, the Sydney Aquarium, and the Sydney Opera House. And he wanted to make sure he tried some grilled kangaroo, crocodile meat and some Vegemite before his trip was over.

10. **It would be a great day for taking the rafts out, Connor decided, as he unlocked the door of his business on yet another sunny day in the town of Moab, Utah.**
Connor first visited Moab when he was in college and his friends persuaded him to join them on a whitewater rafting trip. After that first visit, he returned every year to go rafting on the Colorado River. In college, Connor majored in business, with a concentration in marketing, and he always thought it would be great to own his own business. When he graduated from college, he spent a year as a marketing assistant at a small sporting goods company, specializing in hiking gear. He often went hiking to test out the company's products and realized he preferred to be outside – all the time. Inspiration struck him and he decided to move to Moab, where he started working for a business that offered guided rafting vacations. Over time, he saved enough money to start his own rafting adventure company in Moab, offering one-day trips or longer rafting vacations, helping novices navigate the river and experienced rafters find more challenging adventures. Best of all, however, was being his own boss, spending time outdoors in a town he loved and building a business he really believed in and could watch grow.

Step 2

Answer the following questions:

1. Why did you choose the paragraph you did?

_____

_____

_____

_____

2. What does your answer to question 1 say about you? Your interests? Your experiences?

_____

_____

_____

_____

3. What majors and careers (and not just the obvious ones) can relate to the paragraph you chose to finish reading? Why? **(To answer this question, fill in the following table.)**

Paragraph # _____

Major	Career	Reasons

Group Activity:

Pair up with another student (or work in groups of three). Share what paragraph each of you chose and why. Then, together, write a paragraph based on each of your interests. See how you can make connections between the careers in each paragraph you chose in order to write about a possible career that combines them all.

Activity 19: Your Top Five Dream Jobs: Finding the Real Possibilities

To many, a dream job is what they wanted to do when they were children and had not yet learned the realities and limitations of the "real world." Children are excited and imaginative, allowing them to dream about all sorts of possibilities. Yet, sadly, many adults are not living their dreams. Is that because a dream job is unrealistic? Maybe not. Think back to your past dream jobs, and then think about your current ones. Don't think about reality, or money, or education, or job security; just think about your dreams. When you are ready, write down your top five dream jobs in the box below.

Step 1

My Top Five Dream Jobs

1.

2.

3.

4.

5.

Step 2

Now, decide which two dream jobs you want to continue considering as you complete this exercise.

1._____

2._____

Step 3

Answer the following questions:

1. Why are these two jobs dream jobs for you? Provide as many reasons as possible.

   _____

   _____

   _____

   _____

2. Are there any similarities between the two dream jobs? What are they? If they are very different, what draws you to two completely different dream jobs?

   _____

   _____

   _____

   _____

3. Why are these jobs just dreams for you now? What do you consider the limitations? What do you think you cannot do and why?

_____

_____

_____

_____

4. Now, consider what types of jobs are more realistic for you that are related to these dream jobs. Really think about this. For instance, if one of your dream jobs is to become a professional dancer, what jobs are related to that? (Think about teaching dance, owning a dance studio, designing dancewear, doing public relations for a ballet company or theater, the list goes on.) If you love dance, can you still major in it? What will this degree help you to do? Write down your own related jobs.

_____

_____

_____

_____

5. Now, think about what majors relate to your dream jobs and to your related jobs and why. Dreams can help us choose a major and career. Use your dreams as your guide.

_____

_____

_____

_____

Group Activity:

Share your dream jobs with other students in the class. They may give you more ideas for reaching your goals than you were able to think of yourself!

Activity 20: Completing an Experience Shopping List: What Does It Say about You?

Imagine you have just entered a massive new store where you are able to pick out things you would like to experience (things you want to do that you have not yet done). You can pick out as many experiences as you would like, and any experience you want to have is available. For example, you may pick an experience involving learning how to fly an airplane. Don't be limited by your current reality or whether or not you think you will ever be able to have the experiences. Remember, at this experience store, everything is possible. For instance, have you always wanted to go to France? Do you hope to someday design and build your own house? Have you ever thought it would be exciting to professionally record music with your band and be picked up by a record label? Give this some thought, then write the "shopping list" you will bring with you. Try to list your items in priority order.

My Experience Shopping List	**Things I Want to Do**
1.	
2.	
3.	

4.

5.

6.

7.

8.

Questions about Your "Experience Shopping List"

1. What do these experiences say about you?

_____

_____

_____

_____

2. Why do you want to have these experiences?

_____

_____

_____

_____

3. What can you do now to pave the way toward being able to have some of these experiences?

_____

_____

_____

_____

4. How can courses you are able to take on your campus help you to gain some related experience?

_____

_____

_____

_____

5. Relate at least three of the experiences you listed to possible majors. How are they related?

_____

_____

_____

_____

6. Do any of the experiences listed on your shopping list relate to a possible career? How?

_____

_____

_____

_____

Group Activity:

Share some of the experiences on your list. Give each other ideas about how to have those experiences and how those experiences link to possible majors and careers.

Activity 21: Either/Or: Making Decisions Now to Make Future Decisions

Did you ever think that you might have difficulty choosing a major in the future because you just have difficulty making decisions? Many of us do. Sometimes it is because we have too many decisions, and sometimes it is for fear of making the wrong decisions or committing to only one decision. Yet, you can make deciding easier through practice. Making decisions now can help you prepare for making more difficult decisions in the future.

Step 1

This decision-making activity gives you some practice with this task and gives you only two choices for each category. While you may not have many choices, in the end, your answers may help you learn more about yourself, which, in turn, may help provide you with more information for choosing a major. From each of the pair of items below, you must choose one or the other. Have some fun with this.

1. Hamburger or veggie burger _____

2. Action movie or romantic comedy _____

3. Walk to class or drive across campus _____

4. Dressed up or casual _____

5. Summer or winter _____

6. Rock or country music _____

7. Morning or night _____

8. Writing or typing _____

9. Roller coasters or bumper cars _____

10. Cell phone call or text message _____

Step 2

Think about what these choices say about you. Here are some thoughts to get you started:

If you prefer to walk to class, are you more physically active? Would you mind sitting behind a desk all day? Do you need to move? Do you need to be outside?

If you prefer night to day, what jobs are available at night? What about evening news programs, medicine, jobs that give you a flexible schedule?

If you prefer bumper cars to roller coasters, do you prefer to be in control? Do you enjoy being in the "driver's seat"? Are you competitive?

Now, answer the following questions:

1. What do your choices say about you? What do they say about what you enjoy? What do they say about what you value?

_____

_____

_____

_____

2. Can you relate your choices to possible majors/careers? Think creatively here!

_____

_____

_____

_____

Group Activity:

Get into small groups. Find out how many choices you have in common, then help each other relate these choices to possible majors and careers.

Conclusion

Now that you have completed the activities in this section of the workbook, reflect on what you have learned about yourself. You can use this knowledge as you continue to search for majors that may be right for you. Remember that you want to find out what you love to do and what feels right in terms of who you are. Looking at this first will make finding the right major and career much easier than picking a major, starting a career, and then hoping you love it! Use what you know about yourself now as you work on the activities in Section IV, which will guide you to searching for the majors and careers you will love in places you may never have thought to look before.

Section IV
Discovering Majors and Careers in New Places

Activity 22: Finding a Career in the Newspaper: A Current Events Treasure Hunt

"Finding careers in the newspaper" does not involve scanning the classifieds. It involves actually reading news articles and, while keeping up with current events, finding out what careers are related to people involved in the news stories. You may find out about careers you never even knew existed – or about new careers made necessary because of what is going on in the world. Reading the newspaper is a great way to stay informed, to understand how what you learn in class is related to what goes on in the "outside world" and to improve your reading and critical thinking skills. It is also a great place to discover a major by discovering real-life jobs and careers that really interest you.

For example, the devastating aftermath of Hurricane Katrina was chronicled in every newspaper, magazine and television news show. Also, there were people working on the front lines and behind the scenes from many different fields: rescue and medical personnel, construction workers, politicians, charities, the military. When you followed the news of the hurricane, did you pay close attention to the "who" as well as the "what"? If not, you may have missed learning about the people and the career fields playing an integral role in the response to the hurricane. Here is an interesting (and not obvious) example: Many historic buildings were destroyed in the hurricane, and collections of art from museums, galleries, and artists' studios were washed away. However, many pieces of art have been found, covered with mud and salt water, ripped or broken. While recovering art was obviously not a top priority in the immediate aftermath of Katrina, people eventually began to locate some of the damaged art and that is where art restorers came into the picture. There are many private companies and organizations involved in the restoration of artwork. They employ people with degrees in such fields as art history, fine arts, and conservation. Many of the valuable works of art damaged by Hurricane Katrina are now being restored. If you did not know that, you missed an opportunity to see how a degree in fine arts, for instance, can lead you to doing something other than trying to sell your own artwork. A student who was interested in art history and thought that her options were teaching or museum work was quite surprised and excited about this other career possibility. You too can discover a career in the newspaper by following the steps below!

1. Find a news article (from a newspaper, magazine, or news web site), read it, and bring a copy to class. It should be as current as possible and focus on an area that interests you.

2. Answer the following questions:

    a. What is the article about? (Be as specific as possible.)

    _____

    _____

    _____

    _____

b.   Now answer the *5 w's* of journalism:

Who?

_____

What?

_____

Where?

_____

When?

_____

Why?

_____

c.   Why did you choose this article?

_____

_____

_____

_____

d.   Now focus on the "who": What people are cited in the article?

_____

_____

_____

_____

    e.   What does each person have to do with the story?

_____

_____

_____

_____

    f.   What career/job do you think each person has?

_____

_____

_____

_____

    g.   What majors do you think each person could have had in order to pursue their current field?

_____

_____

_____

_____

    h.   What else do you want to know?

_____

_____

_____

_____

Group Activity:

1. Get into small groups and share your articles as well as your answers to the questions. Each member should contribute any additional ideas they may have about your article as well.

2. After each small group meets, write careers found in the articles on the board. A full class discussion should include information about the connection between the careers, the current event/article topic, and possible majors.

Activity 23: What's Wrong with This Picture?: Reality Versus Fiction in Movie and TV Careers

A movie or television critic writes reviews of current movies or television shows that may appear in a newspaper, online site, or on television. He or she writes about such things as how well the movie or show may represent the genre, the quality of the acting, the cinematography, costumes, humor, entertainment value, or plausibility of the plot. You may have found yourself being a movie or television critic when talking with your friends. Everyone has his or her own opinions about what makes good or believable entertainment.

As you watch movies and television shows, you are often required to suspend your disbelief in order to focus on the entertainment value. But what is real and what is not? The *Mission Impossible* movies, for example, showcase some very high-tech gadgets used to catch criminals or to perform tasks that may not otherwise be possible. We probably all know that many of these "gadgets" do not exist in real life. In the television show *24*, the agents who work for the Counter Terrorist Unit are often able to retrieve data from computers, cell phones, and other devices instantaneously. Is everything realistic? Does all the technology currently exist? Obviously, realism often paves the way for fiction for entertainment's sake. The same my also be true of the characters you have come to love in your favorite movies and television shows. Take, for example, the careers of many of these characters. Are they real careers? If so, in real life, how might these characters be able to actually obtain the jobs that they hold?

Television shows and movies can introduce us to careers and get us interested in a particular field. Many people became interested in forensic science, for instance, because of the television show *CSI*. Likewise, the movie *Jerry Maguire* introduced many people to the job of a sports agent. Medical shows such as *House* may exaggerate the number of unusual, rare, and highly interesting cases the doctors have the opportunity to treat in order to keep the show exciting. The same may be true of the types of cases lawyers get on such shows as *Law & Order*. All this makes for good entertainment. You can learn a lot along the way, however, as long as you are able to connect what you see on the screen to reality and can then assess your own interests and abilities to see if careers you have come to love on TV or in the movies actually exist and are right for you. You can start to determine whether or not a career you learned about on television or in the movies is right for you by looking at what the day-to-day life is like of people in such a career (in real life – not on television!), then make some decisions from there.

Think about two of your favorite television shows or movies. Write the titles below:

1._____

2._____

What do you like about these movies or television shows?

_____

_____

_____

_____

Now, for each television show or movie you listed, identify at least two major characters and their job titles/careers:

(Movie or TV show 1)

Character 1   _____

Career   _____

Character 2   _____

Career   _____

(Movie or TV show 2)

Character 3   _____

Career   _____

Character 4   _____

Career   _____

Now it is time to do some research through the library, your career services office, and reliable Internet resources. For two of the careers you identified above, complete the following questions:

Career of Character 1 _____

1. Is this a real career? Were you able to confirm that this career exists?

_____

_____

_____

_____

2. If not, skip to question 6. If so, what did you find in your research about the skills and education required for this career?

_____

_____

_____

_____

3. What is it like to be in this career? What is the lifestyle? The day-to-day responsibilities? The pros and cons of the profession?

_____

_____

_____

_____

4. What is the outlook for this career field? Are jobs expected to increase or decrease in availability? Why? Where are most of the jobs expected to be?

_____

_____

_____

_____

5. What is the salary range for this career? The typical starting salary?

_____

_____

_____

_____

6. If you did not find this to be an actual career that may be available to you, what careers are related? How? Then go back and answer questions 2-5 for the related career.

_____

_____

_____

_____

Career of Character 2 _____

1. Is this a real career? Were you able to confirm that this career exists?

_____

_____

_____

2. If not, skip to question 6. If so, what did you find in your research about the skills and education required for this career?

_____

_____

_____

_____

3. What is it like to be in this career? What is the lifestyle? The day-to-
    day responsibilities? The pros and cons of the profession?

    _____

    _____

    _____

    _____

4. What is the outlook for this career field? Are jobs expected to
    increase or decrease in availability? Why? Where are most of the
    jobs expected to be?

    _____

    _____

    _____

    _____

5. What is the salary range for this career? The typical starting salary?

    _____

    _____

    _____

    _____

6. If you did not find this to be an actual career that may be available to you, what careers are related? How? Then go back and answer questions 2-5 for the related career.

_____

_____

_____

_____

Follow-up questions:

Can you see yourself in any of these careers? Why or why not?

_____

_____

_____

_____

If so, what majors do you think would help you get there and why?

_____

_____

_____

_____

Group Activity:

Prepare a short presentation to share with a small group or the whole class. Share what you found and provide handouts and/or visuals. The more you can learn from each other the better!

Activity 24: What Does This Person Do? (Creating a Mini Encyclopedia of Careers You May Never Knew Existed)

Sometimes students remain undecided about a major or career because they do not know all of the options available to them, or they may have a very traditional view of careers available to them. This activity is designed to help you see that there are many careers out there that may fit your personality, interests, and skills. You just need to find out about them!

Step 1: Read the job titles that appear below. Which ones sound interesting to you? Which ones would you like to research?

Animal Behaviorist	Magazine Stylist
Radiation	Fingerprint Analyzer
Physicist	Forensic Entomologist
Court Reporter	Human Rights Advocate
Technical Writer	Hydrologist
Life Coach	International Aid Worker
Sommelier	Editor

Step 2: Choose 4 job titles to research. (Be sure to use reputable sources from the library, your career services office, or the Internet.) Fill out the following table for the job titles you choose. Also, research a job title not listed, but one you may have heard of and in which you may be interested.

Variation: Get into a small group and decide who will research what job titles (so that all job titles will be covered). Each person should do the research for his or her assigned job titles, then the small group reconvenes to share what each member has found. Each person in the group can then complete his or her mini encyclopedia by writing down what other people have found. Then, the members of the group can discuss what jobs they found most interesting and why.

Jobs You May Never Knew Existed (or know little about)

Job Title	What the person actually does on a daily basis	What skills the person needs for the job	The education required to enter the profession

Step 3: When you have completed filling in the above chart, answer the following questions:

1. Which job did you find the most interesting and why?

   _____

   _____

   _____

   _____

2. Do you think any of the jobs are a realistic fit for you? Why or why not?

   _____

   _____

   _____

   _____

3. What jobs can you think of that are related to the ones you researched? What other fields may be related?

   _____

   _____

   _____

   _____

4. What other majors do you think can lead a person to the jobs you
    researched? Why?

_____

_____

_____

_____

5. What else have you learned from completing this activity?

_____

_____

_____

_____

Group Activity:

In small groups, create a poster representing some of the careers and
information you gathered about them so that your classmates can learn
from what you found.

Activity 25: Studying into a Major: Linking How You Study to What You Might Like to Do

Answer the following questions. Be honest about yourself.

1. It is Monday and you have a big history test on Thursday that will cover two chapters. How will you study for it? When will you start?

    _____

    _____

    _____

    _____

2. You have five chapters to read in your psychology textbook in two days. What will you do? Will you read everything? Will you take notes? Will you highlight or annotate the text? Will you skim for just the important information? Explain your reading process.

    _____

    _____

    _____

    _____

3. Your friends suggest forming a study group for biology. Would you agree or not? Why? If you did become a part of the study group, how would you like to see it run? Who would do what? How often would you meet? If you did not join the group, how would you study?

    _____

    _____

_____

_____

4. It is Wednesday and you have a paper due on Friday. Is your paper already done? Are you working on it right now? Do you have a rough draft but need to revise it? Have you even started it yet? Explain your answer.

_____

_____

_____

_____

5. You have assignments in three classes: some math problems, a biology chapter to read, and a short essay to complete for literature. Would you most likely get your work done in your own room in your residence hall? Would you prefer to be in the campus coffee shop where music is playing and people are talking? Would it be better for you to be in the library? Can you think of a different environment in which you would be more likely to complete your work? Explain your answer.

_____

_____

_____

_____

6. Do you consider yourself a morning person or a night owl? How does this impact how and when you study?

_____

_____

_____

_____

Part I:

Review your answers to the previous questions. Your answers are telling you about how you like to study, the conditions in which you study best, and even when you are best able to get work done.

Look at the following chart. This chart was completed by Brian, a student who has discovered what works for him in terms of when, how, and where he likes to get work done. Brian thrives on the stress of completing projects at the last minute. He enjoys working with other people and will often study in groups for tests and exams. He is a night owl because that is when he is at his best, but he can pull himself out of bed when he has to. He has also found that he prefers working in the student union building or in the coffee shop on campus, where there is always music playing, people talking or tapping on their laptops, or a television blaring the news or an afternoon talk show. Look at how he completed his chart, and some ideas he had about linking his ideal working and study conditions to majors and careers.

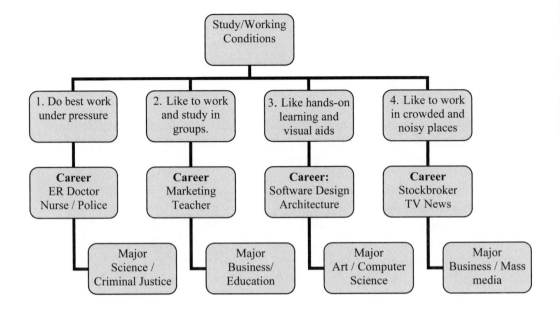

Complete the following chart based on what your learned about yourself from your answers.

1. In the four boxes in the second tier of the chart, write four of your most important working and studying conditions.
2. In the third tier, link each of these conditions to conditions that would be similar in particular careers.
3. In the fourth tier, think about majors that you relate to the career and working conditions in the second and third tiers.

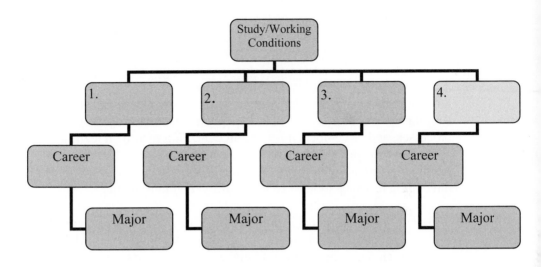

Obviously, just because you may thrive on stress does not mean you will be able to be an emergency room doctor or nurse. You also need the science skills, for instance. But if you love science but do not handle stress or working with people well, you may be better off in a laboratory or research setting. This is why knowing how you best learn and under what conditions you best learn can be another way to start figuring out what you want to do.

Part 2:

Read the following passage as if you were preparing to answer questions in class or to take a quiz the next day (Do whatever you might do to a text when you have to remember information):

Learning Styles

Students can benefit from knowing about their own learning styles. A learning style is best described as the way a person best takes in, processes, and remembers information. Knowing their own learning styles can help students save time and energy while also learning and retaining information in the most efficient and effective ways. There are three basic learning styles: visual, auditory, and kinesthetic.

- A visual learner is someone who processes information through spatial relationships and associations. Visual learners who utilize their learning style would make outlines, charts, or concept maps of information; draw pictures to represent terms or concepts, put information on note cards to look at over and over; and seek out classes in which professors utilize PowerPoint, charts, slides, and videos.
- An auditory learner processes information through listening and discussing. Auditory learners do best when they tape-record lectures or record themselves reading their notes and listening to them again for review, study with a partner or group of students to discuss information, and ask each other questions and review the answers.
- A kinesthetic learner is someone who learns through actions and physical movements his or her body makes. Kinesthetic learners do well when they write material down (some rewrite or type their notes), walk around while studying or memorizing materials, and take breaks to burn off stress or energy through some sort of exercise.

Few students have only one learning style; more often, students learn best with a combination of the learning styles, although one style may be dominant. The important thing is for students to learn about their own learning styles by taking an inventory and then utilizing their learning styles to do well academically. A visual learner who does nothing but listen in order to review material is not going to remember the information very well, while an auditory learner who only reads over notes or a text is doing himself or herself a disservice by not utilizing a strength that could make study time more efficient and productive.

Part 3:

Look back at what you did while you were reading and studying this passage in order to remember it for a class or quiz.

Describe what you did when you were reading the passage and after you read the passage.

_____

_____

_____

_____

What does this say about you?

_____

_____

_____

_____

Part 4:

If possible, complete a brief learning styles inventory. With information you have about yourself as a learner, complete the chart below.

1. In the first box, write your predominant learning style.

2. In the four boxes on the second tier, write some of the things you do to learn and study information based on your learning style.

3. In the four boxes on the third tier, write down some possible jobs or careers that might match how you learn and process information.

4. Finally, in the four boxes in the last tier, write possible majors you link with learning activities and possible jobs/careers.

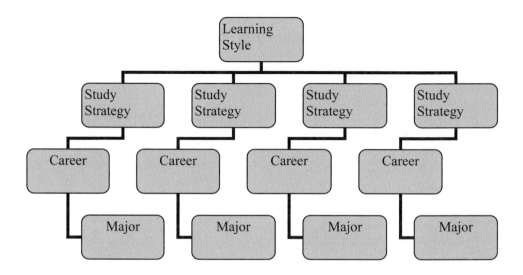

How you best learn and your ideal condition for learning will not lead you directly to a major or career, but this information does say a lot about you. The more you know about yourself, the better you will be able to choose the path that is right for you. If you are a hands-on person and like to see tangible, finished products, you may not get as much satisfaction out of teaching, for example, than you might from designing furniture. When you teach, the finished product, the rewards, are much more abstract. On the other hand, if you are a people person and love to study in groups, then you may not be very happy as an accountant whose time is spent more with numbers than with interacting with people. If you thrive best when able to do long-range planning and working on a project over time, you may find that the last-minute world of print or broadcast journalism is not for you. Learning how you learn can certainly help you succeed in college, but it can also help you decide what to do in college and just what career path may best suit you.

Group Activity:

Get into small groups based on your study preferences. You can share tips and ideas about how each of you related study preferences and majors and careers.

Activity 26: How about Hobbies? (Where They Can Lead)

Golfing, working on cars, cooking, hiking, playing chess, collecting coins, writing music or poetry, building models, sewing, knitting, playing video games, reading a good book. What do all of these things have in common? They are hobbies – things people often do just for fun.

You may be sitting in class thinking that you can't wait for the weekend, when you will finally have free time to take that daylong hike in the nearby state park, get together with your friends to play video games, or write some new music with your band. You all have hobbies, but do you think of them only as things you do when you do not have to work? What about thinking about hobbies as work? Perhaps not in the most obvious ways, such as turning a hobby like golfing into a career as a professional golfer, but in ways that allow you to use the skills and apply things you love to do to realistic careers that are a good fit for you. Let's think about golfing again. What do you need to be a good golfer? Patience? Coordination? The ability to strategize and think ahead? The ability to be objective and keep emotions in check? How about chess? A good chess player also has to be a good strategist, to outthink his or her opponent, to anticipate his or her opponent's next move, to be able to visualize what the board will look like a few moves in the future. Do you know someone who loves to tell jokes or do magic tricks? What is it about that person? Is that person comfortable in front of people, quick witted, creative? What about playing in a band? This hobby is certainly not as individual as golf or chess. People who play in a band need to work well with other people, be comfortable in front of people, be creative, and be willing to take risks.

The point of making these connections is to get you to look at your own hobbies and why you pursue them. Your hobbies say a lot about you. What you like. What talents you have. What skills you have learned. Plus, you enjoy your hobbies, and part of the goal of finding a major and career is to find what you will enjoy on a regular basis.

Step 1: Read the following example

One Hobby	**Many Possible Majors and Careers**

Colin is an avid chess player. It is one of the things he loves to do the most when he is not studying or working. He has played with friends just for fun and has even competed in some local and national chess tournaments. Read how he answered the following questions. You will then answer the same questions yourself.

What is one of your favorite hobbies? Playing chess

What do you like about it?

Chess is very intellectually challenging. I like how I can outwit my opponent. Sometimes I try to disguise a move as something else so that he thinks that my intention is different. When I do this, it is rewarding, especially with a Knight, which I can move in multiple directions. Chess is a mental challenge, not a physical one. I need to be able to change my strategy at a moment's notice when I am outwitted by my opponent. It is a different game every time I play it. Sometimes the game ends after the first few moves, and sometimes a game goes down to the last few pieces on the board. I also love the chess sets themselves. I like the elaborate themed chess sets, such as civil war soldiers or medieval characters and dragons. There is something very artistic about a well-crafted chess set.

What have you learned from it?

I have learned to be very patient and calm, while also trying to come up with ways to outwit my opponent. I think I am very good now at reading other players' facial expressions and anticipating what they may do. I have become much better at visualizing the chess board in my head if I make a certain move over another. I have even learned a lot about the history of the game, how chess sets are made, and about various types of chess sets.

What does your hobby say about you?

My hobby says that I am a thinker and very competitive, but not in a physical way. It says that I like the challenge of such a mental game and that I can handle pressure. It says that I can plan ahead and visualize how things may look in the future.

What majors may be related to your hobby and why?

1. Political Science
2. Military History
3. Marketing
4. Urban Planning

All of the above majors help refine and reinforce the skills I have gained from playing chess. Plus, they involve many of the same things that interest me about chess – such as the history, the strategy, the planning.

What careers do you think of now that you completed all the questions above? Why?

1. Politician
2. Historian
3. Military Strategist
4. FBI Agent
5. Urban Planner
6. Business Strategist or Consultant

Step 2:

Complete the following questions about one of your own favorite hobbies.

What is one of your favorite hobbies? What do you like about it?

_____

_____

_____

_____

What have you learned from it?

_____

_____

_____

_____

What does your hobby say about you?

_____

_____

_____

_____

What majors may be related to your hobby and why?

_____

_____

_____

_____

What careers do you think of now that you completed all the questions above? Why?

_____

_____

_____

_____

As you continue on your journey of major and career discovery, do not minimize the importance of what your hobbies say about you and what connections you can make between hobbies, majors, and careers. There are many possibilities.

Group Activity:

Share your hobby with the class or a small group. Then, ask your audience for ideas about how they might link your hobby to possible majors and careers.

Conclusion

Hopefully, the activities in this section helped you to see that there are many places you can search for majors and careers – and you do not have to go very far! As you begin Section V, continue to pay close attention to what you are doing and to what is going on around you. You never know where you may find just the right major for you!

Section V
Writing into a Major

Activity 27: What Activity Helped You the Most?

Now that you are nearing the end of this workbook, take a moment to reflect on the activities you completed. Which one did you find the most helpful in terms of exploring majors?

_____

_____

Why?

_____

_____

_____

_____

_____

Group Activity:

Share what you wrote with a small group of your classmates. Find out what they wrote and what they gained from the activities they chose. You may be able to look at an activity in a new way.

Activity 28: What Have You Learned about Yourself?

The activities in this book were designed to help you learn more about yourself, which, in turn, will help you make better decisions about majors and careers. Take some time to reflect on what you have learned about yourself from completing the activities in this workbook.

To do so, answer the following questions:

1. You came to college without a declared major. Now that you have completed the activities in this workbook, how do you feel about being undeclared? Do you still feel it was a good choice? Why or why not? Are you more concerned or less concerned about being undeclared now? After completing these activities, what do you think you need to do now to continue your journey to choosing a major?

_____

_____

_____

_____

_____

2. Through activities in this workbook, you have spent some time
    reflecting on what you value. If you had to decide on the most
    important thing that you value in a major and career, what would that
    be? How do you now go about finding majors and careers that
    connect to your values?

    _____

    _____

    _____

    _____

    _____

3. How do you feel now about "dream jobs"? What do your dream jobs
    say about you, and what can you do to discover ways to connect your
    dreams to your reality?

    _____

    _____

    _____

    _____

    _____

4. How are your hobbies, study habits, and personal preferences related
    to major and career choice? Be as specific as possible, and discuss
    how you will use what you know about yourself to continue to
    explore majors and careers.

    _____

    _____

    _____

_____

_____

Group Activity:

Share what you wrote with a small group of your classmates. Ask them to give you additional advice based on the information you shared. Each group member should take turns sharing and giving advice.

Activity 29: What Have You Learned about Majors?

The activities in this book were designed to help you on your journey toward choosing a major that is right for you. Hopefully, you learned more about majors along the way than you knew before.

Part 1:
Answer the following questions:

1. What stereotypes about majors and careers do you feel you have now overcome? Why?

_____

_____

_____

_____

_____

2. How important is a major? How does it define what you do? How does it not define what you do?

_____

_____

_____

_____

_____

3. What is more important: a major or experience? Explain your
    answer.

    _____

    _____

    _____

    _____

    _____

4. What is the value of taking general liberal arts courses in college?

    _____

    _____

    _____

    _____

    _____

5. How can different majors lead you to the same career? How do
    identical majors lead people to different careers?

    _____

    _____

    _____

    _____

    _____

Part 2:

Choose two majors that you are interested in right now and that your college or university offers. Ask yourself the following questions, and then write your answers in the space provided.

1. What are the requirements for me to declare this major? (GPA, prerequisite courses, etc.?)

    _____

    _____

    _____

    _____

2. What type of science and math courses do I need to take in this major?

    _____

    _____

    _____

    _____

3. How many writing courses do I need to complete this major? What are they?

    _____

    _____

    _____

    _____

4. Do I need to take a foreign language for this major? If so, how many
    courses do I need in the language?

    _____

    _____

    _____

    _____

    _____

5. Do the courses I need to take for this major seem to match my
    strengths and interests? Why or why not?

    _____

    _____

    _____

    _____

6. How many years will it take me to graduate?

    _____

7. Will I need a graduate degree to pursue fields related to my chosen
    major? If so, what types of degrees might I need?

    _____

    _____

    _____

    _____

    _____

8. If I can't get into the major of my choice because of requirements, do I have a second choice major that is related? How is this major related to my first choice? What can I do with this major that is similar?

_____

_____

_____

_____

_____

9. What other questions do you have about the major? Write them here, and then find the answers.

_____

_____

_____

_____

_____

Group Activity:

As a class, write what learned about the majors you researched on the board. Discuss what surprises you about the majors and what interests you the most. Ask questions!

Activity 30: What Have You Learned about Careers?

1. Identify a few careers you learned about though the activities in this workbook that you never knew about before:

_____

_____

_____

_____

_____

2.   Which one interests you the most? Why?

_____

_____

_____

_____

3.   What career(s) are you interested in researching further? Why?

_____

_____

_____

_____

4.   How can experience in one career lead you to another one? How do
     people successfully make career changes?

_____

_____

_____

_____

_____

5. How can you find a career you will really love? What can you do
   now to find a career you will love?

_____

_____

_____

_____

6. How are majors and careers connected?

_____

_____

_____

_____

Group Activity:

In small groups, create posters that illustrate your answers to question 6.
Be creative.

Activity 31: A Personal Inventory of Possible Majors and Careers

Step 1:
Complete the table below by writing down all majors you are considering now, or might consider, in the left column, then writing the reasons you are considering those majors in the right column.

Majors under Consideration	Reasons

Step 2:
Now, in the left column, write some of the majors in which you are most interested, then, in the right column write some careers you believe are related to each of the majors.

Majors under Consideration	Possible Related Careers

Conclusion

Think about these questions: What are your top two possible majors right now? Why? What more do you want to know about them?

_____

_____

_____

_____

Section VI
Where Do You Go from Here?

Activity 32: Conducting Research and Gaining Experience

This workbook is just the beginning of your journey. Many of you may still be deciding on a major, and that is fine. While you do not have all the time in the world to pick a major (and you cannot graduate without a major!), you can still work with your advisor to choose the right classes and continue to explore all the majors and minors your college or university has to offer. Perhaps you are ready to declare a major, but even if you are, you should still learn as much as possible about what you might want to do with that major after you graduate. No matter where you are right now on your journey toward choosing a major, you need to continue to conduct research and gain valuable experience.

Part 1:

Here are some things you can do right now:

1. **Find a professor** in the department of the major you are interested in pursuing. Ask him or her the following questions (write the answers in the spaces below):

- How did you get into this field?

_____

_____

_____

_____

- What do you like about your field?

_____

_____

_____

_____

- What can I do with a major in _____?

_____

_____

_____

_____

- What courses can I take now that would help me decide if this major is right for me?

_____

_____

_____

_____

2. **Find a student** in the major you are considering. Ask him or her the following questions (write the answers in the spaces below):

- How did you decide on this major?

_____

_____

_____

_____

- What do you like about being in this major?

_____

_____

_____

_____

- What do you dislike about being in this major?

_____

_____

_____

_____

- What types of courses do you have to take in this major?

_____

_____

_____

_____

- Is help available when you need it?

_____

_____

_____

_____

- What types of opportunities does the department give you to gain experience in the field?

_____

_____

_____

_____

3. **Find an organization on your campus** that is related to a major you are interested. Get involved. This is a great way to see if you like what the major is all about. Write down the names of organizations or clubs on campus that you are interested in joining and why:

_____

_____

_____

_____

4. **Find a job on or off campus** that relates to majors or careers you
    might be interested in. What types of related jobs are available on
    campus and off? Write down how each job you are interested in may
    help you in your choice of a major or in career exploration:

    _____

    _____

    _____

    _____

5. **Volunteer.** You will be glad that you did, and you will learn a lot
    about possible careers that may be right for you. Write down some of
    the volunteer opportunities available to you through your campus
    and why you might be interested in them as they relate to major and
    career exploration:

    _____

    _____

    _____

    _____

6. What else can you do now?

_____

_____

_____

_____

Part 2:

Here are some questions to ask. Find the answers by talking to people in the field, visiting your career services office or the library, and finding reputable web sites.

1. What is the average starting salary for someone in a field I am interested in pursuing?

_____

_____

_____

_____

2. What type of hours would I be working? Would I have traditional hours, or might I have to work nights and weekends?

_____

_____

_____

_____

3. Where are the jobs in the fields in which I am interested? Will I have
    to move? Will I have to live in an environment totally different from
    the one in which I grew up?

    _____

    _____

    _____

    _____

4. What does the future hold for careers in which I am interested? Is
    there growth predicted in these areas? Are jobs in the fields in which
    I am interested expected to decline or increase? Why?

    _____

    _____

    _____

    _____

    _____

Activity 33: Thinking about Job Shadowing

One way to find out more about careers you might be interested in,
which, in turn, could help you gain more information for choosing the
right major, is to job shadow. Job shadowing involves spending time
with a professional in a field of interest and watching what he or she does
on the job. You do not actually do the job, but you get to watch,
firsthand, what the person does in a career in which you have some
interest. Job shadowing is the best way to really see what someone does
every day on the job. You are not reading a book or just talking to people
about what they do – you are actually in the workplace, watching the
action. Job shadow as many different people as possible if you are
considering several career fields. Start by asking people you know if they
can help you contact someone in a field in which you are interested. You

can also talk with your professors and the staff in your career service office. You may also find that alumni are ready and willing to have students job shadow them as well. It may take some effort on your part, but it is well worth it!

Make a list of jobs/career fields in which you would like to find someone to job shadow.

1. _____

2. _____

3. _____

4. _____

5. _____

6. _____

Why would you like to job shadow in these areas?

_____

_____

_____

_____

Write down a plan for finding an opportunity to job shadow.

_____

_____

_____

_____

_____

_____

Activity 34: Thinking about Internships

Internships are different from job shadowing because in an internship you are able to actually work at a company or organization with supervision from someone at the job site as well as someone from your campus. An internship is a great opportunity to help you decide if a major and career is right for you. An internship will allow you to try something new without making the commitment of a full-time job. You can apply what you learned in the classroom to the "real world' while also discovering what you really want to do.

You may be able to earn college credit for internships, and you may even get paid. The most important goal with an internship, however, is the experience, which can help you decide what career you want to pursue while also making you more marketable when you apply for jobs when you graduate. Experience counts!

As an intern, you will most likely be assigned to a mentor who will act as a teacher and a guide, while also providing supervision when you are given projects to complete on your own.

There are many places to learn about internship opportunities. Here are some of them:

1. The department of the major or minor in which you have an interest
2. Professors
3. The career services office at your college or university
4. The alumni office at your college or university
5. Company web sites
6. Friends and family

Think about what types of companies or organizations you might be interested in having an internship with in the future. Then, explain why.

_____

_____

_____

_____

_____

_____

Research at least three current internship opportunities available to students on your campus that you find interesting. Describe the internships below and discuss why you might be interested in those internships.

_____

_____

_____

_____

_____

_____

Things to do now to get ready to apply for an internship:

1. Write or polish up your resume. Get assistance from the career services office on your campus.

2. Practice your interviewing skills. (Some campuses offer workshops on improving your interviewing skills – if yours does, attend one! If not, practice with a friend, professor, or family member.)

3. Secure recommendations from professors. (This is very important. You should begin now to form good relationships with your professors so that you can learn from them, and they will know who you are and what you can do.)

4. Keep looking for internship opportunities.

Activity 35: Continuing the Journey (Keeping a "Travel Log")

This may be the end of the workbook, but it is not the end of your journey. Your journey to discovering a major, and then a career path, is ongoing. Sometimes you find information you can use to help you make decisions where and when you least expect it. You may take a course as an elective and find that it leads you to a possible major. Sometimes you meet someone who will tell you the story of his or her own career path and you may want to remember it. Sometimes you will have the opportunity to research specific jobs and learn important facts such as starting salaries and employment opportunities. You may meet someone who does something you never knew you could do and you want to know more about it. Everything you learn can help you decide on the path your want to take in your own life. Keep a log of what you learn along the way. You can come back to what you wrote whenever you need it.

Here are some ideas of what to keep track of:

Some courses I have liked and courses I still hope to take and why:

1._____

_____

2._____

_____

3._____

_____

4. _____

_____

5._____

_____

Some majors and minors I am still considering and why:

1._____

_____

2._____

_____

3._____

_____

4. _____

_____

5._____

_____

Specific jobs I have discovered that sound interesting and what I know about them:

1._____

_____

_____

_____

2._____

_____

_____

_____

3._____

_____

_____

_____

4._____

_____

_____

_____

5._____

_____

_____

_____

Starting salaries, benefits, and work environment for jobs I am interested in:

1._____

_____

_____

_____

2._____

_____

_____

_____

3._____

_____

_____

_____

4._____

_____

_____

_____

5._____

_____

_____

_____

Notes on interesting people I have met and what they do:

_____

_____

_____

_____

_____

_____

_____

_____

Miscellaneous notes from my journey to choosing a major:

_____

_____

_____

_____

_____

_____

_____

_____

Conclusion

Now that you have completed some or all of the 35 ways to discover a major, the process of discovery can continue — in what you do, the people you meet, the classes you take, and the experiences you have. You may have chosen the right major already, and, if not, you will soon. Keep an open mind as your journey continues. You never know what you will discover!

Appendix

Activity 8: "What's My Major?"

Answers:

		Skills gained from Degree: Paragraph #
Donna's Major:	Accounting	5
Ray's Major:	Bible	2
Ken's Major:	Accounting	4
Karen's Major:	Elementary Education	1
Mark's Major:	English	3

Activity 9: Another Round of "What's My Major?" with a Twist

Answers:

Kelly's Major:	Communication Design
Paul's Major:	Journalism
David's Major:	Math

Group Activity 3: Section II

Answers:

1.	Jon Stewart:	Psychology
2.	Oprah Winfrey:	Speech and Drama
3.	Sandra Day O'Connor:	Economics
4.	Robin Williams:	Sociology
5.	Brooke Shields:	French Literature
6.	Yo-Yo Ma:	English Literature
7.	Sally Ride:	Physics and English
8.	Paul Newman:	English